AF143891

BOOK ANALYSIS

Written by Lina Sánchez
Translated by Rebecca Neal

Heart of Darkness

BY JOSEPH CONRAD

JOSEPH CONRAD

ENGLISH WRITER OF POLISH DESCENT

- **Born in Berdichev (Russian Empire, now Ukraine) in 1857.**
- **Died in Bishopsbourne (England) in 1924.**
- **Notable works:**
  - *Lord Jim* (1900), novel
  - *Nostromo* (1904), novel
  - *The Secret Agent* (1907), novel

Joseph Conrad (born Józef Teodor Konrad Korzeniowski) was a sailor and novelist. He was born in Berdichev in modern-day Ukraine, which at that time was a part of the Russian Empire. His parents, who were both activists in the Polish independence movement, died young, leaving Conrad an orphan at the age of 11.

Following his parents' deaths, Conrad was sent to live with his uncle, then spent a year in Lviv before returning to Krakow. In 1874, at the age of just 17, he left for Marseille with the intention of joining the navy before he had even completed his secondary education. Relatively little is known about his first years at sea, but it is believed that he travelled to the Caribbean, attempted suicide following a setback in his personal life, and had links with arms smugglers for the Carlist political faction in Spain.

At the age of 21, when he became a captain in the British merchant navy, he threw himself into writing. He also adopted the name Joseph Conrad, an anglicised version of his birth name, after he acquired British citizenship. Although Conrad spoke fluent French and Russian from a young age, he did not learn English, the language he is known for writing in, until relatively late in life.

Conrad later travelled to the Congo on board a Belgian steamer and witnessed the atrocities committed by the colonisers first-hand. This journey provided the inspiration for his novella *Heart of Darkness*.

Conrad abandoned his naval career when technological developments rendered steamboats obsolete. He continued writing for the rest of his life and enjoyed a successful career, although none of his other works matched the popularity and critical acclaim of *Heart of Darkness*. His work often reflects on human morality and on the instability and vulnerability of the human condition, and has garnered recognition from a number of modernist and colonialist authors, including Rudyard Kipling (British writer, 1865-1936), Henry James (American writer, 1843-1916) and H. G. Wells (English writer, 1866-1946). Conrad's final years were marked by ill health and gambling addiction.

HEART OF DARKNESS

A DISTURBING JOURNEY IN THE COLONIES

- **Genre:** novella
- **Reference edition:** Conrad, J. (1995) *Heart of Darkness & Other Stories*. Ware: Wordsworth.
- **1st edition:** 1899
- **Themes:** madness, savagery, brutality, colonialism

Heart of Darkness is a novella which brims with mystery and symbolism. It tells the story of Charles Marlow, a sailor who is travelling along a tropical river in search of a general named Kurtz. In the course of his journey, he witnesses the atrocities perpetrated by Europeans in Africa and the way that conflict drives humanity to the brink of madness.

Marlow eventually finds Kurtz, whose condition has degenerated, leaving him sick and mad. He is a white governor in black territory, and is seen as a god by the region's indigenous inhabitants.

Marlow is shocked by this discovery and spends Kurtz's final days trying to help him and, above all, to find out how he got into this state. The novella as a whole is an unflinching exploration of colonialism, madness and brutality.

SUMMARY

The cruising yawl the *Nellie* is sailing down the Thames with a group of passengers. The narrator tells us that from this position, they can see the largest and most powerful city in the world: London.

Most of the story is narrated by the *Nellie*'s captain, a former sailor called Marlow, who has sailed the Indian Ocean, the Pacific Ocean and the seas of China. When he was a young man, he visited Africa, where he witnessed the way European colonisers have ravaged the continent first-hand. This journey forms the heart of the narrative.

Marlow tells the rest of the sailors on board the *Nellie* the story of his youth. This story opens when he asks his aunt for help finding a job, and she puts him in touch with a company that is hiring sailors to travel to Africa. He undergoes a somewhat strange medical examination, in which the doctor measures his skull (a reference to the pseudoscience of phrenology) before telling him that he does not believe in the method, as madness comes from inside rather than outside the brain and therefore cannot be measured in this way.

PHRENOLOGY

It is significant that Conrad depicts phrenology in his book. Believers in this pseudoscience thought that key personality traits could be discerned by measuring the dimensions of the head. The discipline has been discredited for over a century, and is highly controversial because it is based on racist premises. Specifically, its development was based on the prevalent belief that Native Americans and black people were naturally lazy and servile, and many of its proponents' real aim was to advance European interests and development.

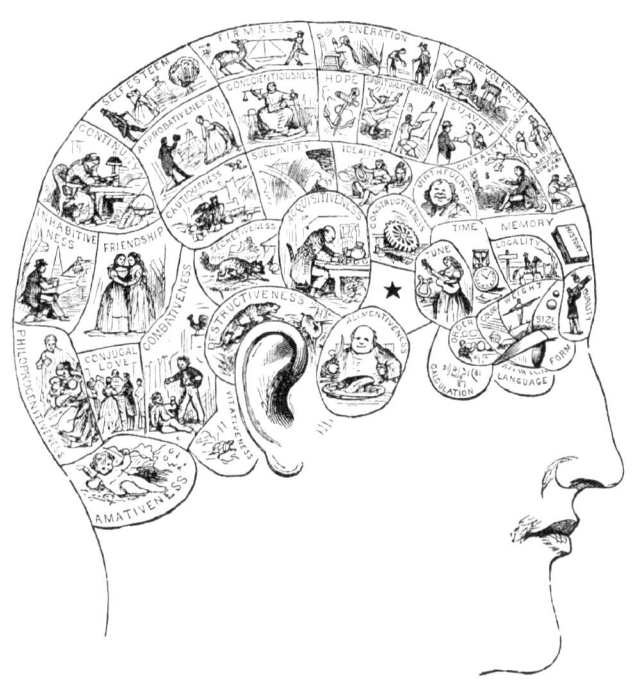

The human faculties according to phrenology.

The young Marlow then sets sail from the Thames and sails down the Atlantic coast until his ship reaches the mouth of a tropical river. His predecessor at the company, a man named Fresleven, was murdered in Africa. It takes him over a month to sail down the river until he reaches the premises of the Company, which deals in ivory. He sees a white man pointing a rifle at several black men, who appear to be slaves. It is a hellish place that is characterised by intense suffering, and explosions resound in the distance.

To make matters worse, the general manager, a miserly man who seems to go out of his way to make Marlow's life harder, tells him that his boat is damaged and that he will have to wait three months for it to be repaired. A well-dressed accountant tells him about a strange man named Kurtz, who has reportedly gone mad, and a young employee tells Marlow to put in a good word for him when he meets this Kurtz. Rumours spread like wildfire through the premises: it is said that Kurtz is quite unwell, and that he left a few months ago and has had no contact with the Company since.

Marlow is given the all clear to leave and gets ready to set out in search of Kurtz.

VOICES IN THE NIGHT-TIME MIST

Marlow finally sets out to look for Kurtz, accompanied by a motley crew of religious pilgrims, soldiers and cannibals. The journey does not go entirely smoothly: in the middle of the night they hear screams and beating drums, and although the travellers know that the noise comes from the natives, they do not know exactly what they are doing.

Marlow's memories of the inhospitable, oppressive atmosphere of the jungle are mingled with his recollections of the stench of hippopotamus meat that the cannibals eat, which rots as they are travelling. When they hear voices in the night, the cannibals are seized by a desire to eat human flesh, but Marlow manages to calm them down.

This section of the narrative features more frequent references to the ivory trade, which is what has drawn the colonists to this part of the world.

Death seems to be lying in wait for the travellers, and as they are approaching the Company's station, which is the last place where Kurtz was seen, a group of natives attack their boat. Even though they only have bows and arrows and the Europeans have rifles, the boat's steersman is hit in the chest and mortally wounded.

The natives flee when Marlow sounds the vessel's steam whistle. He throws the dead man's body overboard so that the cannibals do not eat him, and picks another man to replace him. They set sail, and a strange white man, who is dressed in patchwork clothes that make him look like a harlequin, approaches and tells them that they have nothing to worry about: the natives attacked the boat to protect Kurtz, who is alive.

PARODY IN *THE SIMPSONS*

A group of explorers who are attacked or observed by natives as they cross a river at night has become a common image in popular culture. In the *The Simpsons* episode "Simpson Safari", the eponymous family thinks that they are being attacked by members of an African tribe, who make noise and play music from the riverbank. Homer throws a stone which hits one of them, who then turns to his friend and says that it seems rude to throw stones when they are only trying to greet the visitors. This scene parodies the river journey in the second chapter of *Heart of Darkness*.

"THE HORROR! THE HORROR!"

The man dressed like a harlequin tells Marlow about Kurtz's illness. Kurtz has managed to gain control of the territory, whose inhabitants now follow him as their leader. Marlow is fascinated by this mysterious figure: although it is said that he still seems to speak rationally and is forbearing with the natives, who worship him and grovel before him, the harlequin assures Marlow that Kurtz is mad and is not far from death. He does not say much more, but he too appears to be unbalanced. Night falls over the jungle and everyone goes to sleep.

At midnight, Marlow hears a loud scream and immediately sets about trying to find out where it came from. He follows a recently-made path which leads him to Kurtz. Rather than taking him along with his crew, Marlow takes him back to the town he is governing. In the course of this chapter, Kurtz's madness can be seen on numerous occasions when he screams in the middle of the jungle.

Marlow keeps talking to Kurtz, who gives him some papers during one of their conversations but tells him not to show them to anybody. Kurtz also wakes up in terror in the middle of the night and repeatedly screams "The horror!". After this episode, he dies and a small funeral is organised. The boat returns to the Company's main station, and then to Europe. Marlow jealously guards the documents that Kurtz entrusted to him, but once he gets back to England they are taken from him by journalists and bureaucrats.

In the end, Marlow manages to give Kurtz's fiancée two letters. When she asks him what his last words were, Marlow lies and says her name.

Marlow's story is at an end, and the novel closes with a description of the vast horizon that can be seen from the *Nellie* in London years later.

CHARACTER STUDY

Although the novel does have a number of concrete characters, such as Kurtz, Marlow and the general manager, many of its characters are abstract: the whites, the blacks, the jungle. These abstract characters are not precisely described and are difficult to pin down.

This was a deliberate narrative choice: the fact that there are few well-developed characters with their own names and distinctive personality traits emphasises these characters' power over the masses. Furthermore, the lack of individualised descriptions adds to the impression that the inhabitants of Africa have more in common with the continent's landscapes than with other human beings: they appear to be a mass with no individual identities of their own. The few black characters who are described in greater detail serve to convey the general characteristics of or contrast with the rest.

CHARLIE MARLOW

Charlie Marlow feels most at home on the boat he is sailing on. Unlike his fellow sailors, who are always looking forward to returning home, he is a nomad at heart and soon feels disgusted when he has to spend too much time among people on land. He is a great observer and a wise man who has seen many things that others have not.

Before he meets Kurtz, he is very curious about him: he wants to know how he works, what illness he is suffering from, if he is really mad and, if so, how he ended up that way. When Marlow encounters Kurtz and spends some time with him, he starts feeling as though there is a deep bond between them and believes that he has a brilliant mind, even going so far as to describe him as "a universal genius" (p. 100).

Marlow could also be interpreted as the personification of complete indifference, as very little moves him or stirs his emotions. Sometimes he is amused by the behaviour of one of the black men he is travelling with, but he always seems nihilistic and stoical, as though his entire life were dedicated to constantly observing or sailing.

Some critics have also interpreted Marlow as a representation of the author. He refers to the writing process on more than one occasion, and shares his story with his listeners on the *Nellie*. In spite of his apparent indifference to the world around him, he analyses the events he has witnessed and provides a skilfully crafted, emotional account of his experiences.

KURTZ

Kurtz has been shaped by his passions, giving free rein to even the most primitive of them, and is a fearsome ruler of the hellish environment of the novella.

His greatest gift is his eloquence: he can speak persuasively and with apparent expertise on virtually any subject, and is able to express himself in simple, beautiful, poetic language.

Hubris is not Kurtz's only sin: not only does he set himself up as a deity ruling over his miniature kingdom, but he is also cruel, violent and murderous. He goes out hunting to get his hands on ivory, and his office is decorated with the heads of some of the elephants he has killed on these expeditions. He has an ambivalent relationship with the region's black inhabitants: he has power over them as their leader, but deep down he loathes them and wants to wipe them off the face of the earth.

As Marlow says, Kurtz is a paradoxical figure. For example, "kurtz" is German for short, but the man himself is tall. Furthermore, although in his unparalleled violence and brutality he is the living embodiment of savagery, his mastery of language grants him significant power in "civilised" societies.

His exceptional powers of persuasion and the fact that echoes of his voice can be heard across the jungle raise him to a status that is quasi-divine. Like a god, everyone knows of him, his words serve to answer and justify any questions, and he is perceived as a source of enlightenment.

Although Kurtz's presence is important, it is less significant than his absence from the first two chapters of the novella. He exists through the voices that talk about his genius, his power and the way the territory's indigenous inhabitants adore him. He is seen as a god not just by the natives, but also by anyone who hears him speak or hears others speak about him.

In the second chapter, Marlow is driven purely by his desire to find Kurtz, as though his journey were a pilgrimage. The dichotomy at the heart of the book comes from Kurtz: he is both "a universal genius" and an unhinged killer.

THE HARLEQUIN

This improbable character is Russian, which is surprising given that Russia never established permanent colonies in Africa. He displays a range of often contrasting character traits, and he can be seen as a symbol of all the nations of Europe.

He is the only character who possesses a book (which can be seen as a symbol of European cultural development), which is interesting given that he is depicted as unmotivated, simple and careless. He seems to be captivated by Kurtz, and repeatedly says that he has "enlarged [his] mind" (pp. 82 and 91).

The harlequin is one of the most widely studied and analysed of all the characters in *Heart of*

Darkness. He can be seen as the voice of sanity in the midst of madness, like Sancho Panza in *Don Quixote* (novel by Miguel de Cervantes [Spanish writer, 1547-1616], 1605 and 1615). He is also the only character who has a separate life outside the perverse world of the jungle, which means that he is the only character who can live in the "heart of darkness" without going mad and, by extension, the only truly "good" or "innocent" character. However this character is interpreted, his presence in the novel borders on the improbable or the inexplicable.

THE WHITE CHARACTERS

Although there are numerous white characters in the novella, few of them are depicted as individuals with their own personalities and distinctive traits. Although the others do have some distinguishing features, they are not well-developed as characters, and can be seen as representations of the different kinds of white people who have travelled to the African jungle. Some of the most significant white characters in the novel are analysed below.

Fresleven

Fresleven started off as a peaceful man, but after two years in the jungle, a seemingly trivial event unleashed a darker, more brutal side of his character, and he brought about his own downfall through his violent actions. He is the first white character who is truly aware that he is living in the "heart of darkness", and serves as our first introduction to two key themes in the story: the brutality and madness that reign among the colonisers, and the way that the whites are treated as gods or deities by the black indigenous inhabitants. Fresleven also illustrates two of the most important qualities for surviving in this inhospitable environment, namely charisma and physical resistance to the unforgiving climate and the life-threatening illnesses lying in wait for the explorers.

The doctor

The doctor conducts some routine medical examinations before Marlow leaves for Africa. As well as asking whether mental illness runs in his family, he measures the diameter of his head. At the time the novella was written, it was widely believed that evolution and the superiority of certain groups of humans over others could be proven by measuring the skull and other bones.

The doctor also makes clear that the men who leave for Africa never truly return, either because they physically die or because the experience changes them so drastically that they are never the same afterwards. He also recommends that Marlow stay calm, as calm and rationality are antithetical to brutality and savagery, and are the traits that separate humans from animals.

The general manager

The general manager is inquisitive, envious, fame-hungry, treacherous and petty, and has no real positive qualities to speak of. He may be plotting against Kurtz, and he is ruled by primitive passions which are only tempered by his extreme miserliness. He does not have a clearly defined personality, does not say very much about anything and only hangs on to his position as general manager because of his ability to resist the jungle's brutal climate. In this sense, he can be viewed as the simplest and most primitive of the white characters.

The accountant

The accountant takes great pains to maintain his composure and keep up appearances: his hair is always neatly combed, his clothes are clean and he smells good. Marlow respects his ability to keep dressing as though he is in Europe when he is in the inhospitable jungle.

The women

White women live apart from the men and are shut out of their world, which is where power is concentrated. If they wield any social power (for example when Marlow's aunt uses her connections to get him a job), the men see this as humiliating, as they do not want to be helped by women. Women at this time were seen as untouchable and apart from worldly concerns; instead, they were viewed as passive objects who existed only to be observed.

THE BLACK CHARACTERS

The novella's black characters are viewed as an indistinguishable mass rather than as characters in their own right, with their own names, voices and personalities, which serves to depersonalise them. Furthermore, they are sometimes described in a way that makes them seem more animal then human. Instead of wearing clothes, they partially cover themselves with shapeless, brightly-coloured and often threadbare rags; they wear necklaces and hang amulets and objects related to witchcraft around their necks; and some of them even seem to have horns. All this stands in sharp contrast to the whites, who wear suits and smoke English tobacco. This depersonalisation of the novella's black characters makes it easier to dehumanise them.

In Marlow's descriptions, the black inhabitants of the jungle are depicted as the antithesis of the whites, especially when he sees them for the first time and thinks that what he wants more than anything is not to see them again. Even though they are clearly exhausted and suffering, there is something about them that repulses him. Seeing them as merely an odious mass makes compassion for them impossible. Although the indigenous habitants are not seen as fully human, they are not complete animals either, leaving them in a sort of perverse in-between state. The narrator describes their movements as erratic and compares their behaviour to natural elements:

> "Now and then a boat from the shore gave one a momentary contact with reality. It was paddled by black fellows. You could see from afar the white of their eyeballs glistening. They shouted, sang; their bodies streamed with perspiration; they had faces like grotesque masks – these chaps; but they had bone, muscle, a wild vitality, an intense energy of movement, that was as natural and true as the surf along their coast." (p. 41)

Europe and Africa as depicted in *Heart of Darkness* seem to come from completely different time periods, as the indigenous Africans seem to come from a more primitive time than the more developed Europeans. According to Conrad's depiction, Africans seem to be from an earlier stage of humanity's development, and their vague resemblance to the Europeans only makes them easier for the colonisers to hate. Marlow ponders the relationship between the whites and the blacks when he wonders why the cannibals on board his boat have not eaten the five white men, especially seeing as there is not enough food to go around and hunger has the power to undermine even the strictest morality.

Cannibalism and savagery

For centuries, cannibalism has been used as a sign of "savagery" and as a way of depicted the indigenous inhabitants of newly "discovered" territories as primitive, uncivilised beings. For example, in Christopher Columbus's (Genoese navigator, 1451-1506) earliest diaries, he refers to the indigenous inhabitants of the Americans as beings who eat human flesh.

The term "cannibal" comes from the Arawak languages, which were spoken by indigenous peoples in South America, and originally had the sense of "brave" or "daring", or "strange" or "foreign". Furthermore, although there are some isolated pieces of evidence of populations which carried out cannibalistic rituals on rare occasions, cannibalism is far more widespread in artistic and political representations of the indigenous inhabitants of Africa, Asia and South Africa produced by European colonisers than it ever was in real life.

It is worth adding that the novel's black characters are not perceived as criminals or as enemies of the whites, because this would imply that they were seen as equals in some way, which is clearly not the case. In the first chapter in particular, they are depicted as nothing more than hollow shells, worn down by illness and exhaustion. We can tell that they are alive because they breathe heavily and walk around as if they are very tired, but apart from that they seem utterly lifeless.

In the second chapter, two black characters are referred to more specifically. The first of them stokes the coal that is used to power the steamboat, and is impressive because he knows how to work a boiler, while the second is the steersman. These two characters are "domesticated" versions of the mass of "savages" in the jungle. Significantly, the black characters who approach the river move as part of a pack and are not depicted as individuals. Although the two black characters on the boat are more individualised, Marlow cannot help but see them as humorous figures: "[T]o look at him was as edifying as seeing a dog in a parody of breeches and a feather hat, walking on his hind-legs" (p. 64).

When the steamboat is attacked shortly before reaching Kurtz's quarters, the steersman dies an undignified death when he is hit in the chest by an arrow, and his body is then thrown overboard. Although Marlow watches him die, he does not feel any compassion towards him. He thinks that his death is a shame because he was a good steersman, but his attitude is more reminiscent of the way one would treat a pet, and he is annoyed that his blood has stained his shoes. Indeed, although Marlow does briefly wonder why the black passengers are so outraged when the steersman's body is tossed overboard, most of his attention is devoted to his new shoes and his regret at having to throw them overboard too because it will be impossible to get the bloodstains out. This is one of the most difficult passages of the novella to read, as it illustrates Marlow's complete lack of regard for the black steersman's life, which he sees as less important than a pair of shoes.

THE JUNGLE

The jungle in the novella seems to be a living, breathing entity which conceals savages and their mysterious intentions, and which can leave the white explorers both blind and deaf. It is portrayed as impenetrable, infinite and possibly home to a multitude of subhuman creatures. Entering the jungle makes it difficult for the characters to keep the outside world in their sights and sets them on a path that leads to savagery and madness.

The fact that the jungle is both dense and remote makes it a breeding ground for primitive passions, brutality and violence, and the whites see it as unfit for human habitation.

Although Marlow is affected by the brutality and violence that characterise the jungle, and by the loss of contact with life and death, he never really enters the heart of it. He remains on its outskirts as he sails along the river, and although black Africans attack his steamboat from the banks, he only encounters this brutality briefly instead of being immersed in it.

ANALYSIS

Heart of Darkness is not only famous for its analysis of colonialism and political ambiguity: it is also significant because it serves as something of a bridge between two important literary traditions, namely 19th-century realism and the Modernism of the early 20th century. In this sense, it prefigures the work of James Joyce (Irish author, 1882-1941) and Marcel Proust (French writer, 1871-1922), and is skilfully written to draw the reader into both the literal jungle and the metaphorical "jungles" of the narrative and the narrators' minds.

A narrative jungle

At the time Conrad was writing, a shift in narrative techniques was taking place. Previously, and particularly in the 19th century, the narrators of most texts were omniscient, meaning that they could observe everything in the world and had unbiased insight into their characters' minds.

Honoré de Balzac (French author, 1799-1850), one of the best-known and most influential writers of the 19th century, often used this technique, and his narrators tend to be aware of even the smallest details about the characters and the world around them. In this way, they are seemingly inexhaustible sources of information about topics as diverse as opera, the printing industry, contemporary architecture and the political stances of the various social classes.

However, this is not the case in *Heart of Darkness*, which actually has two narrators who narrate separate sections of the story, with the second narrative fitting inside the first like a Russian doll. The more objective and distant of these two narrators is a sailor on board the *Nellie*, who listens with rapt attention as the captain tells the story of his journey. This narrator describes Marlow and gives us some initial information about his personality.

The second narrator is Marlow himself, who gives a first-person account of his experiences in Africa. He is by turns measured, calm, frightening, fierce and understated, and proves a skilled storyteller. As he is telling his story to a group of sailors, he needs to hold their attention and provide a precise account in a limited period of time.

As such, the boat which is sailing down the Thames serves as the setting for a frame story which introduces the story we are reading, namely the story of a man who was driven mad in Africa. Like the dense, impenetrable jungle, the narrative is packed with meaning and features multiple interwoven stories. *Heart of Darkness* forms part of a long tradition of narratives which use frame stories, including the *One Thousand and One Nights* and Chaucer's (English writer, 1342/3-1400) *The Canterbury Tales* (1387-1400).

A mental jungle

The novella's two narrators are quite different to the archetype established by Balzac. While the French author's narrators had no personality of their own and could see everything that happened, Conrad's narrators are human, and this is reflected in the way they tell their stories: they pay particular attention to certain details and do not know everything about the world around them. Instead, we are given unprecedented insight into their perspectives, weaknesses and use of language. Although we do not find out everything there is to know about African industry, culture, demographics, and so on, as would be the case with one of Balzac's narrators, with Conrad we are taken into the mind of the narrators, who talk about the world around them and their impressions about it, but who do not have a complete, overarching view of it.

Heart of Darkness also stands out for its use of language, which serves to draw us further into Marlow's mind. Numerous critics have argued that the language Conrad uses is linked to the mist that shrouds the jungle, and to the uncertainty and danger that pursue the travellers. It is undeniable that an entirely objective description of this world would prove less brutal and frightening than a description shaped by the thoughts of a man who is slowly going mad.

This process of developing madness can be seen in the fact that the descriptions become stranger as the narrative progresses: the images become vaguer, the sounds become shriller and the space becomes far less precise. This means that the events recounted do not have one single interpretation: instead, the story traces the decline of a mind and a culture, and the exploration of uncharted regions of both the physical world and the human psyche. As the steamboat sails down the river and the terrain becomes increasingly inhospitable, we discover other ways of seeing and describing the world.

Madness

Marlow is on the verge of madness when he is in Kurtz's quarters and realises that the other man has left. When he sets out to look for him, the distant drums beat in time with his heart, as though he has suddenly turned into a leopard stalking its prey through the jungle. In this tense atmosphere, he finds himself face to face with a black man with horns, and knows that there are others nearby:

> "A black figure stood up, strode on long black legs, waving long black arms, across the glow. It had horns – antelope horns, I think – on its head. Some sorcerer, some witch-man, no doubt: it looked fiend-like enough." (p. 93)

The novella's three central themes, namely madness, savagery and brutality, are closely linked. Madness can develop when the characters are bewitched by the "heart of darkness", or when they are overcome by their most primitive passions. When Marlow realises that Kurtz is talking about every topic and every aspect of culture as though they belong to him alone, he starts to understand how the jungle can magnify even the most seemingly insignificant feelings until they are all-encompassing.

The novella also depicts a sort of vicious circle: madness begets brutality, which in turn begets more madness. There are only two possible ways of dealing with the extreme violence depicted in the story: indifference, as embodied by Marlow, and madness. Characters can only remain indifferent in the absence of primitive passions: miserliness, desire for renown and covetousness will lead irrevocably to madness, which will inevitably manifest itself through violence.

After he returns from Africa, Marlow realises that even though whites in Europe enjoy a greater degree of security and technological development, they are also simple in their behaviour and

harbour foolish dreams, which can pave the way
to brutality and madness.

Savagery

Savagery has both physical and temporal ma-
nifestations in the novella. In physical terms, it
can be seen in the descriptions of the indigenous
inhabitants, who appear as a homogenous mass
that seems to have emerged from the earth. The
further into the jungle Marlow travels, the less
rationally he is able to think; his journey and the
power of nature and the river are leading him
towards a more instinctive, animalistic state of
being. In other words, the further the characters
get from "civilisation", the more brutal, irrational
and bloodthirsty their behaviour becomes.

This is reflected in the novella's black characters,
who have always lived in an "uncivilised" land
and are therefore seen as irremediably savage
and incapable of rational thought by the whites.
Instead, they are viewed as entirely governed by
their passions. For example, when the rotting
hippopotamus meat is thrown over the side of
the steamboat, Marlow's first instinct is to wonder why the cannibals did not immediately eat

him and the other passengers, thus illustrating how he views the black passengers as animalistic creatures who are prepared to turn to cannibalism in order to satisfy their hunger.

In temporal terms, savagery is linked to primitiveness. Although the jungle coexists alongside the European world, it seems to come from a different stage in the development of civilisation. Consequently, the journey along the river can also be viewed as a journey back in time. The jungle is a prehistoric location that existed long before the arrival of humans and their culture. However, a short journey by boat can quickly transport the passengers back to civilisation.

Brutality

Brutality is embodied in the novella by Fresleven, who whips the elderly tribal chief because he suspects him of theft. However, this is only the beginning of a chain of escalating brutality. The people who survive in the brutal conditions of the jungle are those who can withstand the harsh climate, and they then turn to violence to maintain their position.

Heart of Darkness also lays bare the brutality of colonialism, as at this time the majority of Africa had been colonised by various European powers. The jungle, where the forces of nature are unremittingly brutal, is a breeding ground for myriad forms of violence. Violence in the novella is also symbolic: episodes such as the death of the steersman, after which Marlow laments his stained shoes and orders that the body be thrown overboard, and images such as the row of heads which line Kurtz's office are extremely violent. The story therefore depicts not just physical violence and destruction, but also the degradation of the human soul. As such, the brutality, bestiality and violence of the jungle can be said to coalesce into something even darker: "[t]he horror!" that becomes Kurtz's dying words.

Colonialism

Heart of Darkness was written in the late 19th century, at a time when views about colonialism were shifting. It was no longer unanimously seen as a civilising mission which aimed to bring culture and progress to every corner of the world; instead, there was increasing awareness of the violence perpetrated against millions of people in Africa, Asia and the Americas by Europeans.

Conrad was influenced by this context, and his novella is more than just an adventure story. It is also an ambivalent political text, which some have seen as foreshadowing later anti-imperialist movements. Specifically, it criticises the injustice, violence and brutality that accompanied the Europeans' exploitation of resources in their colonies around the world.

However, others have accused Conrad himself of racism and imperialism. Notably, the Nigerian writer Chinua Achebe (1930-2013) criticised the novella in his essay "An Image of Africa: Racism in Conrad's *Heart of Darkness*". In this essay, Achebe analyses the ways that the novella's black characters are likened to animals and are seen as an indistinct mass that almost forms part of the landscape, and further asserts that the text is a source of violence that will later be replicated in real life.

FURTHER REFLECTION

SOME QUESTIONS TO THINK ABOUT...

- What forms does colonialism take in the present day?
- Write a short account from the point of view of one of the cannibals on the steamboat.
- Why can it be said that the novel's black characters are depicted as if they were a part of the landscape?
- Do you think that Conrad's writing is racist?
- Have you seen scenes similar to those in the novella elsewhere in popular culture?
- What is the harlequin's function in the novella?
- Can you think of any characters from popular culture who are linked to cannibalism?

We want to hear from you!
Leave a comment on your online library
and share your favourite books on social media!

FURTHER READING

REFERENCE EDITION

- Conrad, J. (1995) *Heart of Darkness & Other Stories*. Ware: Wordsworth.

REFERENCE STUDIES

- Firchow, P. E. (2015) *Envisioning Africa: Racism and Imperialism in Conrad's Heart of Darkness*. Lexington: University Press of Kentucky.

- Watts, C. (2012) *Conrad's Heart of Darkness: A Critical and Contextual Discussion*. Amsterdam: Rodopi.

ADDITIONAL SOURCE

- *Simpson Safari* (2001). The Simpsons. [Television programme]. Fox: 1 April 2001.

RECOMMENDED READING

- Achebe, C. (1977) *An Image of Africa: Racism in Conrad's* Heart of Darkness. Massachusetts Review. 18.

ADAPTATIONS

- *Apocalypse Now.* (1979) [Film]. Francis Ford Coppola. Dir. USA: American Zoetrope.

Bright ≡Summaries.com

More guides to rediscover your love of literature

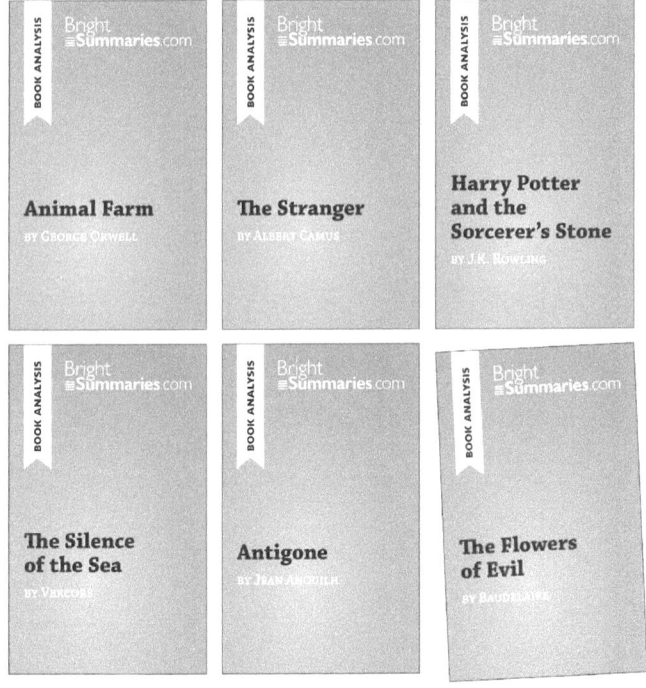

www.brightsummaries.com

www.brightsummaries.com

Ebook EAN: 9782808002141

Paperback EAN: 9782808009324

Legal Deposit: D/2018/12603/225

Cover: © Primento

Digital conception by Primento, the digital partner of publishers.